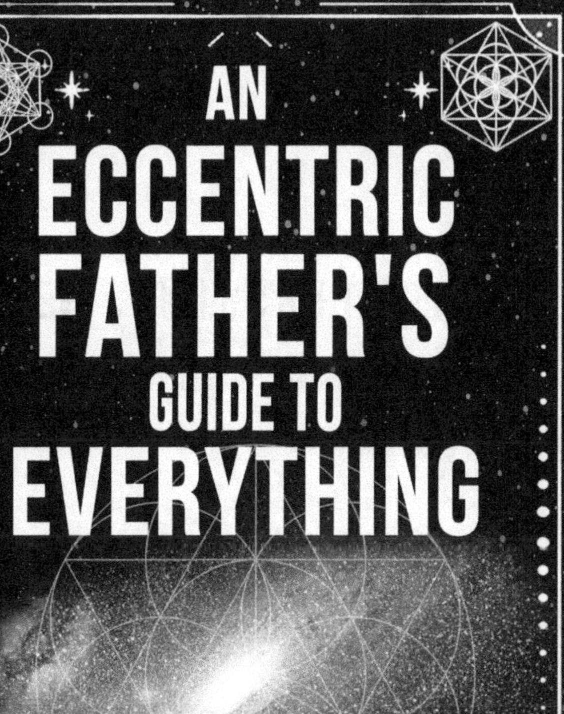
AN
ECCENTRIC
FATHER'S
GUIDE TO
EVERYTHING

ALI KADEN

AN ECCENTRIC FATHER'S GUIDE TO EVERYTHING

Cover concept by Ali Kaden

Editing and cover build by George Verongos

ISBN: 9798336651874

Also by Ali Kaden...

Kali on the Ropes is a gritty psychological thriller about addiction, redemption, and the struggle for a new life. Blending Christian and Hindu spirituality, the story delves into the power of faith and sacrifice in the face of darkness. Aarya's battle stretches far beyond the boxing ring as she confronts the brutal reality of sex slavery in the impoverished streets of Kolkata.

Visit www.AliKadenBooks.com

Contents

Preface 1

1. Seeing Things as They Are.................................... 5

2. The Physical Dimension.................................... 17

3. Religion and Ideology 31

4. Integrating Body, Mind, and Soul 47

5. Ancient Wisdom and Modern Insights............ 59

6. The Fabric of Reality 73

7. Who Am I? 83

Preface

I wrote this book primarily for my daughter as a personal legacy, but I eagerly welcome anyone else to read it who might find value in its pages.

My dear daughter, this book is for you. Here, I will try to tell you all the things I wish someone had told me. Many people go through their entire lives not fully understanding who or what they are until they face an existential crisis. It's taken me a long time to come to my own understanding of what this life is all about, and I'd like to share it with you.

There are many things that society doesn't teach us that we need to know. The educational system didn't teach me the meaning of life, but it also failed to mention some practical things like credit scores, mortgages, and life insurance, which would have been useful for someone to understand going out to face the modern world. But this book isn't about credit scores and life insurance. It's about the very fundamental truth of our reality, who we really are, and the deeper meaning of existence.

There is so much I wish to share with you that I hope will enrich your life. While I don't have all the answers, my innate curiosity has always driven me to explore and question everything, so I know a little about a lot of things. By the time you're old enough to read this, you'll know that about me.

This book is also a guide for you, partly because you're growing up in a multinational, multireligious environment—like my own upbringing, which I found quite confusing at times. It's hard to know what to believe, which philosophies to subscribe to, and how to find one's own place in the world. I'm writing this so you don't get lost in the noise or indoctrinated with nonsense. This book will discuss religion, science, philosophy, and the concept of God, but it's not meant to be a religious book. It is not meant to convince you to "believe" in anything, but instead to see things as they are.

Some would look at me and see all sorts of contradictions. I've been described by a close friend as "dichotomous." I work in real estate, but I also write books like this. I'm a Muslim man who married a Christian woman, and I have a Sanskrit mantra tattooed on my arm. Your mother shows you a beautiful side of religion, where you see communal prayer, community involvement, and service to others. With me, you get someone more out of the box. My daily spiritual practices are diverse, drawing upon multiple religions and traditions. To some, that seems contradictory, even wrong, but it makes perfect sense to me.

Growing up between the diverse cultures of Egypt and the United States, I had the unique opportunity to view life through distinctly different perspectives and religious traditions. It always intrigued me how people could strongly identify with one viewpoint while, halfway around the world, others held a completely contrary perspective with equal conviction. Rather than aligning myself firmly with one group,

I became a student of perspectives. One crucial insight I've gained is that truth is often paradoxical—no single perspective can be absolutely true.

I enjoy learning from all world religions, and I also love science, history, and metaphysical studies. This book has a touch of all that. I hope what you read here elevates your consciousness and your love to the next level.

~ Ali Kaden

1. Seeing Things as They Are

Dear daughter, or anyone else reading this book, rather than simply accepting this or that philosophy, I want you to know that the key to truly understanding the world is to simply see things as they are. Having lived in multiple countries, I've observed that people, no matter where they are, often adopt beliefs more for a sense of belonging than out of a sincere desire to find truth. This could be due to strong nationalistic sentiments or fervent religious beliefs. I've never been satisfied with just accepting an ideology without question. Life is too complex to be confined to a single religion or philosophy claimed to be "the best." I do not believe dogmatism leads to true understanding. Instead, I believe in the practice of cultivating awareness. This is the essential lesson of this book.

Unmasking Education and Cultural Biases

When I was twelve, my family moved back to Egypt and, in addition to my schoolwork, I also had an Arabic language and Islamic religion tutor who came to our home on weekends. During one lesson, he discussed the concept of heaven and hell. He confidently stated that those who did not believe in God were destined for hell. Curious, I asked him about people who had never heard of God, like perhaps those born on remote islands or in strict communist countries. If God was benevolent and kind, how could he punish those who've never heard the message? My tutor struggled to give a satisfactory answer because his beliefs were simply inherited, with no real understanding or critical thinking on his part. It was then that I realized...my tutor was an idiot.

In that moment, I saw how people can cling to their beliefs out of habit or the need for acceptance rather than true understanding. I knew I just couldn't be that way. While those who follow dogma blindly can still be wonderful people, it's in my nature to seek my own truths.

The idea of accepting what is told to us as truth with little questioning is prevalent in religion, but also in our educational systems. Education is a funny thing because learning is an endless frontier, but today's educational systems sell a narrow prescription for life. Our economy is built around the manufactured ineptness public education facilitates. They set us up to compete with our peers, seek accolades, and rush towards a concept of success that has us overworked and feeling empty all for the good of our employer. Conventional wisdom can be so twisted that it will set us on a path that is sure to result in depression, then turn around and offer us the pill to treat it. Often, even our parents can't teach us all we need to know to thrive.

Society values intellectual achievements too highly. People are pushed to excel academically, then professionally, showcasing their intelligence through good grades, high IQ scores, salaries, and yearly bonuses. But being well-educated or professionally successful doesn't always mean someone is well-rounded, healthy, or truly happy. This intense focus on intellectual and monetary success is why many people work extremely hard, only to end up dissatisfied later in life.

The world is this way because human civilization highly values strength and intelligence. These ideals are reinforced by religious and educational institutions, reflecting dominant paradigms is our way of thinking. Historically, human survival depended on physical strength and mental acuity. For thousands of years, our ancestors struggled to obtain necessities like food, water, and shelter, and often didn't live past the age of thirty-five. Being strong and smart offered clear survival advantages, leading societies to idealize these qualities over other vital ones.

Society has also historically favored masculine traits, largely because qualities like strength and intelligence were traditionally associated with males. This emphasis continues to shape our world—most global leaders are male, and in some theologies, religious figures are strictly male, too.

In modern professional environments, women often feel compelled to embody masculine traits, downplaying their own femininity to progress. However, this approach neglects the value of traits typically associated with femininity. In religion and in culture, the power to create and sustain life has always been associated with the feminine aspect. This is why we often think of compassion, nurturing, and emotional intelligence as feminine attributes, and they are critical for a balanced and healthy society. This balance of masculine and feminine is something that is needed on a societal level, but also within each individual. Acknowledging and valuing these attributes is crucial for fostering a more equitable and harmonious world.

Overcoming the Mind's Limitations

Intellect is not the most crucial aspect of our consciousness. When it comes to storing information, our brains are not limitless. There is a finite amount of information that our minds can hold. In today's world, we are often encouraged to specialize in something because mastering every field is unrealistic. The education system rewards those who can absorb large amounts of knowledge, perform well on tests, and earn degrees. Society praises individuals who outperform their peers with their earning capacity.

To exclusively idolize and reward intellect in this way fails to consider the full human experience. Love is not experienced through the intellect. Contentment in life is not achieved solely within the mind. A full human experience involves being connected to all aspects of oneself.

Our bodies and brains are the result of millions of years of evolution. If the world values the ability to store vast amounts of information, then we should be more impressed with our bodies than our minds. The human body holds a wealth of knowledge that far surpasses what our minds can comprehend. We do not consciously control the digestion of food, the absorption of oxygen in our lungs, regulating our heartbeat, or the cleansing of blood by our liver. We look the way we do because our body remembers all ancestors, going back to the very start of life on earth. Until recently, mainstream science thought less than ten percent of our DNA was functioning and used primarily as a blueprint for physical development. Only now is research being conducted to unravel what information is in that other ninety percent.

We are the most advanced species on the planet when it comes to consciousness and self-awareness. Yet, many people are troubled by their psychological processes, whether it is anxiety, depression, or simply a failure to summon appropriate will power to accomplish tasks. Therefore, it should seem that having control over the mind is more advantageous for living a full life than merely remembering information or wielding a sharp intellect. To be complete, we need to harmonize all facets of ourselves, mastering our emotions, and being fully present in our bodies.

I can see that during times when I relied too much on my intellect, expecting intelligence to carry me to where I wanted to go, I was neither happy nor successful by my standards. In my commercial real estate career, the greatest successes and joys did not come because I showed someone else I was smart. When I led with numbers and facts, and was emotionally distant, hiding behind my intellect, I bored people. That's not good for businesses. The best outcomes came as a result of me being centered and genuine. Maintaining a pleasantness within myself and in my interactions opened more doors and created far more opportunities than complex financial modeling, business acumen, or the ability to store a lot of information in my brain.

Cultivating Awareness

The most valuable advice I can offer is to cultivate awareness, which is a central theme of this book. No matter what challenges or situations we encounter in life, it's crucial to see the world as it is. This is not just about looking outwards, but also about being connected with every part of ourselves. This involves not just depending on our intellect or adhering strictly to any one belief system or philosophy, but instead embracing a broad, open-minded approach to life. Being curious about everything helps us see things as they are, with less subjective influence.

The source of much human suffering lies in our tendency to overly attach ourselves to one aspect of our being, rather than embracing our entire selves. When we define ourselves solely by one thing, like our intellect, we leave ourselves vulnerable to pain and disappointment. When I show my daughter affection, it is not done through my intellect alone. We love with our entire being and cannot live a fulfilling life if we suppress the complexity and richness of our complete self.

When individuals depend too heavily on a single aspect of their being to face life's challenges, they frequently run into obstacles. Someone who relies solely on their intellect may try to tackle emotional issues with pure logic. This approach can lead to frustration and stagnation, as they struggle to truly process and move past their feelings. Similarly, a person who is overly focused on their intellectual capabilities might find it difficult to empathize or genuinely connect with others, resulting in feelings of loneliness and disconnection. On the other hand, individuals who lean entirely on physical strength or endurance to deal with life might push themselves to exhaustion, ignoring the mental and emotional signals that call for rest or reflection. Those who adhere rigidly to a specific ideology may find themselves unable to adapt to new situations or consider alternative viewpoints. In Buddhism, it is taught that attachment leads to suffering.

It's very common for human beings to create suffering for themselves, using their own psychological processes. Jagadish Vasudev, known as the mystic Sadhguru, is a respected spiritual teacher from India that I love to listen to. In one of his talks, he uses a vivid analogy to illustrate the suffering created by the mind.

There is a hypothetical person whose arm is uncontrollably punching them in the face. Sadhguru points out that most of us would consider that person quite unwell. Yet mentally, people beat themselves up with negative thoughts every single day, and we consider that normal. We accept it as inevitable because we're conditioned to believe that our thoughts are who we are, when they're just a small part of who we are.

This is why the practice of awareness is so important. Learning to detach ourselves from the constant identification with our thoughts can greatly enhance our experience. When we start to see life as dynamic rather than static, we stop allowing our psychological processes to create suffering, which is life changing.

Meditation: The Path to Peace

Being rooted in awareness is not a mental exercise; it involves letting go of thoughts and simply existing in the present moment. For as long as I can remember, I've been drawn to seeking the truth in everything. I've always enjoyed exploring spirituality and God, but not strictly within the confines of science or organized religion. My true interest lies in personal experience, rather than relying on others' interpretations. As I grew older, I discovered meditation and realized that true understanding cannot be attained through knowledge alone but also through the practice of meditation.

When I started exploring meditation, a simple explanation that resonated with me was that the goal is to lengthen the space between thoughts. At first, it might only be a few seconds between thoughts, but with practice, the gaps get wider. The trick is to let thoughts rise and fall without engaging with them, and eventually, the mind quiets down. I focus on my breath or visualize light to stay centered. As the space between thoughts becomes wider, awareness grows. With less clutter in the mind, we can see and experience the world more clearly, without projecting our thoughts and feelings onto it. More importantly, we begin to identify ourselves not with our thoughts, but with the silent observer within—the part of ourselves that can watch our thoughts and is therefore greater. Our true self.

Imagine trying to meditate in a forest by focusing solely on a single tree without getting distracted by your thoughts. Even with something as simple as focusing on a tree, taking in the intricate details of its leaves and bark, most people find themselves caught up in their inner dialogue and unable to stay fully present. Our fast-paced world has conditioned us to constantly seek stimulation, leaving little time for stillness. As a result, we struggle to control our compulsive thought processes. The tree, of course, is just a metaphor for life. Observing the tree means being fully present in the world.

People who regularly practice meditation understand how easy it is to be pulled away from the present moment by thoughts of the past or worries about the future. They strive to value the present moment over the constant chatter in their minds because they know that an unchecked mind leads to suffering. We all have the potential for greatness, but when we let our thoughts control us, we fall into distraction. A quiet mind, on the other hand, is peaceful and effective. Cultivating mental stillness allows us to perceive and appreciate the world as it is. As a parent, the most important lesson I have to offer is just this: The more you remain in a state of awareness, the better and more magical your life will be.

Embracing the "I Am"

In the teachings of the Abrahamic monotheistic faiths, when God says, "I am," it is often understood as simply a confirmation of His existence. However, this statement is much deeper; It signifies that one aspect of God is pure consciousness.

We, too, have pure consciousness within us. The silent and watchful consciousness within is our true self. This is the part that should be identified as "I" or "me." It is our "I am."

When our mind is calm, the power of our consciousness grows. This is what awareness truly is. The term "seer" reflects this state—it denotes someone who sees deeply, rooted in the present moment, and fully engaged with life. Special insights and abilities flow from this state.

The state of awareness is like being in love. Love is not calculated, computed, or based on specific instructions. It simply exists within us and flows outward. The more we cultivate it, the more it grows.

Many individuals who follow religions often become consumed with ideology rather than focusing on their own inner experiences. They might believe that adhering to strict rules is the key to living a good life or that being part of a specific religion is the only "right" choice in the eyes of God. This can lead to confusing "believing" with "being." I have found that spirituality is not something to simply understand but rather to feel and experience. Those who practice awareness will find that right actions flow naturally from within, without the need to muster willpower or desperately cling to a sense of morality. I'm not suggesting that morality doesn't matter, only that dwelling on it excessively is not the path to goodness.

Throughout this book, I will mention God and religion, but not to persuade you toward any particular path. To me, labels like Muslim, Christian, Hindu, and Buddhist are only as meaningful as the sincerity of the person practicing their faith. As a Muslim, I find it more meaningful that the word itself in Arabic means "one who surrenders" rather than just a follower of a specific faith. The ultimate surrender is to the pure consciousness within, where we find our connection to God.

2. The Physical Dimension

We live in a world that we can perceive through our senses, a world that is tangible and material. Science aims to understand these tangible elements and measure them to explain reality. However, I urge you to not confuse measuring with knowing. The data we collect from experiments and observations are just numbers and theories, and they are pieces of a much larger puzzle. While we operate within a reality governed by physical laws and observable forms, our existence extends far beyond what our five senses can detect, or our brain can conceptualize.

Physicality is just one dimension of all that exists. The idea of multidimensionality is not just for mystics, it is a crucial aspect of our existence that can be explored and understood. Through cultivating a state of awareness, we can expand our perception beyond the limitations of the physical world. There are deeper truths of existence beyond what can be seen.

Instead of only focusing on one type of science or the other, let's try to look at things as they are. Everything that exists reflects the order and repeating patterns of our universe. This intricately connected structure of reality points to a creative intelligence expressed in everything. Whether we look at an atom, or a solar system, we will see a grand design at work, marked by perfection in balance and symmetry. As Einstein famously expressed:

"My religiosity consists of a humble admiration of the infinitely superior spirit that reveals itself in the little that we, with our weak and transitory understanding, can comprehend of reality."

Studying a little science might lead you to atheism, but studying a lot of science reveals the presence of something greater at work.

Grasping Duality

The physical dimension is created through duality. Every aspect of our experience and understanding is manifested through polarities. This means that all phenomena can be measured and comprehended within a framework of opposites—hot and cold, good and bad, up and down, big and small, proton and electron, happy and sad, and countless other contrasting pairs. These polarities are seemingly infinite, providing the context for our minds to understand life.

Duality is evident not only in the physical world but also within us and in how we intellectually engage with various fields of study. In physics, duality helps us understand phenomena ranging from the vastness of the cosmos to the tiny world of subatomic particles. It allows us to comprehend concepts like large and small, near and far, and the physical properties of matter. Psychology examines the spectrum of human emotions and mental states, from joy to sadness and from sanity to insanity. Concepts like good and evil, God and Satan, heaven and hell, highlight complex spiritual ideas, shaping religious beliefs.

There are opposing, or positive and negative, elements in all things, as symbolized by the yin and yang. From sexual reproduction, which combines masculine and feminine DNA to create new life, to the phases of day and night on Earth, to the subatomic level, where protons and electrons carry opposite charges—everything physical is born from dualistic interaction. In trying to understand the world around us, our mind divides ideas into smaller parts, looking for these inherent dualities.

In the physical world, everything has its opposite, but these opposites point towards an absolute source. When we study the vastness of space, we naturally wonder about the size of the universe, which turns out to be ever-expanding and therefore infinite. In human affairs, our search for truth leads us to ideals that seem beyond our reach—like perfect justice or absolute fairness—qualities often attributed to a divine creator that no one person could uphold or embody. We are born and we die, but we contemplate an eternal afterlife. The structure of the world compels us to seek something absolute beyond our immediate reality.

Rising Above Duality

The great spiritual teachings of the world suggest that duality is an illusion to be transcended. In Islam, the concept of "Tawhid," the oneness of God, encourages believers to see past the apparent dualities of life and recognize a singular divine source. Judaism discusses balancing justice and mercy, symbolizing the need to transcend opposites to achieve harmony. Christianity presents the Trinity, which unites God and man, overcoming worldly duality. Buddhism teaches the Middle Way, a path that avoids extremes, like asceticism or indulgence. In Hinduism, the figure of Ganesh, the elephant god with one tusk instead of two, represents overcoming duality to achieve enlightenment.

The mind inherently experiences duality, constantly oscillating between opposites such as past and future, or good and bad. This creates conflict and separation in our thoughts and emotions. Awareness, however, is pure observation beyond judgment and attachment. Through meditation, we cultivate this awareness, allowing us to see the transient nature of our mental states. This helps us transcend the mind's dualities and align with a deeper reality. For example, if we say killing is universally wrong, why don't we consider it evil when a lion hunts and kills a zebra? Because knowing what a lion is allows one to transcend dualistic conclusions. There is always a deeper truth beyond absolutes.

If absolutes are not true, then no one thing can be completely one way or the other. This means that the truth about any given matter must be paradoxical. The size of a marble seems small to us but immense to a tick. This duality, where something can be both small and large, highlights the contradictions inherent in our understanding of the world.

We can never fully grasp absolutes, so we must accept paradoxical truths. Light behaves as both a particle and a wave; time can feel fast or slow depending on our perception, and what is considered morally right in one culture may be deemed wrong in another. We'll never find the highest, lowest, best, or worst of anything in a world of infinite variation. Our intellectual pursuits are therefore limited because thoughts are born of duality. We do not derive awareness of how things are from thought, but rather from the very act of seeing.

The practice of awareness is essential for transcending duality in the mind. Awareness allows us to hold two opposites in our consciousness at the same time because we can see how a thing is both near and far, depending on the perspective.

Consider the phases of day and night on Earth. Depending on which side of the planet we're on, we experience either day or night. However, if we view Earth from far away in space, we would be able to see both day and night happening simultaneously across different parts of the planet. A broader perspective, free from attachments to absolutes, leads to a more profound understanding of the world.

Understanding Dimensions

Through cultivating awareness, we can transcend duality in the mind and begin to experience the multidimensionality of reality, revealing that the physical world is just one aspect of a much broader existence. Consider dimensions like the different layers of our planet—the atmosphere, stratosphere, and terrestrial layer, each with its own distinct characteristics. No single layer is representative of the entire earth. We must consider all the layers, and more, to understand what our planet is.

The physical world is part of a multidimensional whole, and so are we. Events that we perceive to happen one way resonate through different dimensions that are less tangible and not consciously perceived. In science, particularly quantum mechanics, evidence that particles exist in multiple states simultaneously supports the idea of multidimensionality. A particle can be in two places at once or spin in opposite directions at the same time, suggesting that our universe is not confined to what we can just see and touch.

In religious and spiritual contexts, dimensions are viewed as spiritual realms that go beyond our physical existence, connecting to a larger cosmic or divine plan. Traditional teachings sometimes depict heaven and earth as separate places—a "here" and a "there." However, a different perspective suggests that there is no "there," only "here," because everything is interconnected. The visible and invisible realms are intricately woven together, forming a unified reality where the boundaries between here and there dissolve.

Throughout history, there are cases of people who can predict future events, communicate with spirits, and access elevated states of consciousness. They could see past one dimension into another, acquiring what we would consider supernatural knowledge.

The Five Elements

The physical world is a product of duality, with opposing currents flowing through all things. This duality takes shape in many forms—atoms and electrons, magnetic and electric forces, masculine and feminine energies. It comprises the tangible matter and intangible energy that we perceive through the five elements. These elements represent the observable aspects of existence—what we can see, hear, and touch. Scientifically speaking, these elements consist of molecules made up of atoms. The arrangement of subatomic particles within these atoms determines their type, which in turn defines the element. By altering the arrangement of atoms and molecules, different compounds and elements are created.

The four classical elements are earth, air, fire, and water. Water is adaptable and essential for life, taking the form of whatever it fills, demonstrating its flexibility and persistence in various states—liquid, solid, and gas. Earth is solid, providing a stable ground to stand on and serving as the foundation for all physical structures. Air, though invisible, is crucial, filling our lungs and circulating vital oxygen, permeating every environment we encounter. Fire is raw energy, its heat and light transforming anything it touches, driving chemical reactions and changes in state.

These elements are dynamic, constantly interacting and transforming. Solid rocks erode into soil, which supports plant growth. Water evaporates from oceans, forms clouds, and falls as rain, nourishing the land. Leaves and organic matter decompose, enriching the soil and creating a cycle of life and renewal. Forest fires clear dead vegetation and release nutrients back into the soil, fostering new growth. These interconnected processes highlight the continuous interplay of earth, air, fire, and water in the physical world we perceive.

Our bodies are composed of the same elements found in nature. Our bones and tissues, rich in carbon, provide structure similar to the earth beneath our feet. We rely on air for every breath, bringing oxygen into our lungs. Our digestive system acts as an internal fire, converting the food we eat into energy. Water circulates through our veins, transporting essential nutrients and genetic information in our blood. These elements are present within us, just as they are in the earth and the sun that sustain life.

The fifth element is known by different names in different cultures. It is a mystical, invisible force that underlies and connects all of existence. In Greek philosophy, it is known as ether, the essence of creation and a pure celestial substance filling the universe. Modern science refers to it as dark matter, an invisible substance that comprises about 85% of the universe's mass, detectable only through its gravitational effects. In Eastern spirituality, it is called Akash, representing the all-encompassing space or ether through which energy flows.

Most of what we perceive as tangible reality is empty space. Atoms have a dense nucleus at the center, surrounded by electrons that occupy a vast area, making the atom predominantly empty. Similarly, outer space is largely empty, with enormous distances separating planets, stars, and galaxies. This highlights the fact that both the microscopic and macroscopic realms are composed mostly of voids, despite their appearance of solidity.

The concept of nothingness or voids is often misunderstood as something negative or devoid of value. However, in philosophical terms, nothingness is not an empty void but the foundation of all potentiality. It is the space where infinite possibilities can emerge.

The Role of Consciousness in Reality

We've explored the significance of awareness in understanding reality, but it isn't as simple as that because our consciousness has the ability to change matter. Our consciousness shapes the reality around us, highlighting a vital link between our inner states and the external world.

In 1801, physicist Thomas Young conducted what is known as the double-slit experiment, which significantly advanced our understanding of the nature of light. In this experiment, he shined light through two closely spaced slits, and the resulting pattern displayed on a screen showed interference and diffraction patterns, characteristic of wavelike behavior. This finding was pivotal because it demonstrated that light could act as a wave, challenging the prevailing notion that light consisted solely of particles.

With advances in quantum mechanics, similar double-slit experiments were conducted using electrons and other particles,

Remarkably, these particles also exhibited wavelike properties, forming interference patterns when passed through the slits. However, a curious phenomenon emerged—when the electrons were observed, they behaved like particles. When unobserved, they behaved like waves. This shift from wavelike to particle-like behavior showed that consciousness influences matter. In other words, the world we see is partially created by our seeing it.

Everything we perceive as solid and distinct is part of an interconnected pool of energy. Consider the idea that every time you leave your house, it ceases to exist in its solid form and transforms into a blur of energy, only to reassemble into the familiar structure of your home upon your return. Our consciousness and observation actively construct the reality we experience.

Einstein's theory of relativity, encapsulated in the famous equation $E=mc^2$, also illustrates the multidimensionality of the universe by showing that energy and mass are interchangeable, with the speed of light as a constant. His equation shows how similar mass and energy are. Similarly, Einstein introduced the concept of space-time, blending time and space into a unified continuum. Space time, like particles, is influenced and changes depending on the observer and their location.

Even our individual experiences of time and space are relative. Our emotional states influence how we perceive time— a happy moment can pass quickly, while a period of sadness may seem to drag on forever. In my experience, it is by improving the quality of my consciousness through awareness that I can perceive the connection between the mind and the outer world. I have come to understand that every moment matters, every thought creates ripples of experience, and every aspect of our lives is being co-created by us.

For my daughter, I hope these insights give her a sense of ownership of her experience, because it is through changing ourselves that we can affect real change in the world.

Understanding Universal Laws

As mentioned earlier, traditional education fails to provide a holistic view of reality. This limitation is evident in our specialized, compartmentalized approach to learning. In medicine, for example, every body part has its own specialist, reflecting a larger system that prefers to view components in isolation rather than in connection. One doctor will look at your knee, another will examine your ears, yet another your liver, yet hardly any of them will take one full look at you.

During my teenage years, my interest in school waned significantly because the curriculum seemed utterly detached from real life. Tasks like calculating the area of a trapezoid or memorizing historical dates without understanding their real-world impact appeared meaningless to me. School felt like a bubble, where everyone agreed to play by made-up rules, where the ability to memorize information and pass tests held more merit than being centered as an individual.

This year, my daughter is starting kindergarten. In considering her education, I value her ability to sit in the present moment, in awareness, and to recognize the interconnectedness of all things, above any grades or accolades she might earn. When we are aware of ourselves and the world around us, we are engaged in our learning because everything is relevant. In awareness, nothing is mundane. If only I had known that even a trapezoid is connected to the universal fabric of reality, my school experiences would have been vastly different growing up.

In many world religions, there's a common belief that earthly events are mirrored in a spiritual realm. This concept is encapsulated in the saying "as above, so below," indicating that the universe operates under consistent laws and patterns across all dimensions. The study of universal laws and what some call sacred geometry seeks to uncover these fundamental consistencies.

Over 2,300 years ago, Plato introduced the concept now known as the platonic solids. He described five perfectly symmetrical three-dimensional shapes, each corresponding to one of the classical elements: the tetrahedron for fire, the cube for earth, the octahedron for air, the icosahedron for water, and the dodecahedron for ether or the cosmos. Fascinatingly, these shapes find parallels in modern molecular chemistry. For example, methane molecules, linked to fire, have a tetrahedral structure. Pyrite crystals, associated with earth, naturally form cubes. In certain liquids, clusters resembling the icosahedral shape are linked to water.

In the study of cymatics, scientists have discovered that sound frequencies can create geometric patterns in substances like sand, water, and other media. This suggests a close relationship between energy frequencies and geometric shapes. From a different perspective, these geometric patterns might influence the formation of matter itself.

Perfect mathematical ratios and concepts, like pi, the Fibonacci sequence, and the golden ratio, could in essence precede the formation of matter, possibly originating from a higher order or divine realm. It is not surprising that people have created monuments and art to reflect these divine patterns for thousands of years. Structures like the Great Pyramids and works of art like Leonardo da Vinci's Vitruvian Man embody these universal principles of sacred geometry, preserving and transmitting them through time.

3. Religion and Ideology

This chapter discusses religion but does not prescribe any particular one. While I understand that people often feel the need to honor the specific culture they come from, speaking about religion in absolutes has always seemed limiting to me. True spiritual seeking, in my view, is a deeply personal, internal journey. Religions are not the truth—they merely attempt to point toward it. There will always be those who claim their way is the only true way, but I urge you to be wary of such simplistic and ignorant assertions.

In all religions, the creator is described as infinite, omnipotent, and omnipresent. When people set rigid boundaries around their beliefs and declare them as absolute truths, they unintentionally restrict the limitless nature of God. Claiming any ideology as the end-all be-all of spiritual seeking elevates the ideology above the personal experience of the divine, making some idea or concept more important than the experience of life itself.

Ideology vs. True Spirituality

Whether living in Egypt or the US, I noticed that many people simply inherited their beliefs without integrating them into their personal experience. It's common in many faiths to believe that heaven is exclusive to their followers, and people accept this without question. But how can one know if they were born in the right religion, or converted to the right faith to earn this salvation?

The idea of a one true faith reduces human spirituality to a matter of mere membership rather than deep and universal experience. If God is really merciful, kind, and compassionate, there couldn't be favoritism toward any religion, language, culture, or group, because so many would be forsaken.

Claiming religious exclusivity often leads to looking down on other beliefs and practices. Other religions are viewed as false, as well as things that fall under new age spirituality, like astrology and tarot cards. Followers will cite scriptures to justify rejecting other cultures, alluding to their practices as being explicitly forbidden or evil because of some interpretation of an ancient text. This fear of what is deemed evil can lead to harm, as history has tragically shown. The burning of so-called witches—not just in Salem, but globally is an example of religious fear turning into paranoia. The intolerance bred by religious exclusivity has often caused more harm than good.

Even religions that champion love, compassion, mercy, and charity can lose their essence when they become rigid ideologies. Once spirituality becomes dogmatic, it often strays from its true spirit. For example, imagine we create a religion centered around the principle of "love." Initially, it attracts like-minded individuals, and everything seems harmonious. However, the real test comes when we meet people who disagree with our views. If our response is to exclude, judge, or alienate them, our religion of love contradicts itself by failing to embody the very principles it promotes.

Judging and excluding others contradicts the teachings of many great religious figures, like Moses, Jesus, Buddha, and Muhammad, who all emphasized unity and love. Sadly, it's easy for people to fall into the trap of creating divisions while thinking they are being righteous, often remaining ignorant of religious traditions outside their own. Even the kindest people can make this mistake if they worship ideology at the expense of open-mindedness and compassion. This leads to the travesty of hurting and alienating others in the name of God.

As a father, it is the esoteric teachings that I wish to share with my daughter, because through their lens, one can look at all the religions and see the same message, shared from the same singular divine source, expressed through various messengers, prophets, and gurus through the ages. Messages get distorted over time, like playing a game of telephone, where one person whispers a secret to another and that person whispers to another. What happens eventually is that the last person to hear the secret receives a completely different message than the original one. The same has happened in religion. However, the truth is that all religions originate from a singular source, and if we look closely, we'll see the common thread running through all of them.

The Harmony of Faiths

It's a travesty that many religious leaders today remain entrenched in narrow interpretations of their ideologies. This approach makes them impediments to humanity achieving a global consciousness. They prioritize rigid adherence to specific beliefs over a holistic embrace of human spirituality. By doing so, they act more like narrow-minded cheerleaders for their faiths rather than guides toward a broader, more inclusive understanding of spirituality.

I've heard religious figures answer some of life's most important questions with the answer: "God is mysterious." I find this very frustrating, because I believe all answers can be found across the world's spiritual traditions, but it requires one to be open and step outside singular ideologies. For example, if you ask many religious people, "Why did God create disease or poverty?" they'll tell you God works in mysterious ways, or that it's the work of the devil. But if you go to the Eastern faiths, you'll find a treasure trove of answers on these subjects that find resonance in both science and with inner intuition.

Of course, most people in a religion do not typically want to search other faiths for answers, but this has always been my way. I appreciate sowing religions together at the seams. One of the most inspiring experiences I had was during college, when I spent three-months volunteering with the Missionaries of Charity in Calcutta. People from across the globe came to volunteer side by side to help the poor, regardless of their religious backgrounds. We served Buddhists, Hindus, Muslims, and more. It was particularly moving to me to see how the sisters respected everyone's faith, even in death. When the elderly or infirm died in their care, the sisters honored their burial rites. They did not impose their traditions on others.

Another beautiful example of religious acceptance and cooperation that I witnessed came from my Jesuit college professor. He was a devout Catholic priest, yet his openness and reverence for all faiths reflected his profound love for God, free from spiritual arrogance. In the class I took with him, Intercultural Autobiography, he spoke with deep respect for Islam while we studied Malcolm X and similarly about Hinduism during our discussions on Gandhi. For him, as it is for me, human spirituality had nothing to do with affiliations and exclusivity. It is about the collective human experience in all religions, throughout our entire history going back to the first discovered cave paintings, to when our ancient ancestors first sought to honor something that seemed magical outside of themselves.

In contrast, one of the worst and most upsetting religious interactions I had was during a conversation with a Christian pastor. Despite having a PhD in theology and working in Cambridge, Massachusetts—a melting pot of diverse backgrounds and faiths—he displayed a surprisingly superficial grasp of religions other than his own. During our conversation, despite knowing my religious background, he insisted that Jesus was the only way and dismissed all other religious paths as simply being wrong. It was shocking to see a religious leader so deeply entrenched in narrow ideology speak in such absolutes.

His insistence on the exclusivity of his beliefs showed that his education was more about affirming his biases than exploring spiritual truths. I'd argue he didn't truly understand his own faith, either. Despite Jesus preaching non-judgment, this pastor had no problem saying that two-thirds of the world's population was wrong about God, yet he displayed shocking ignorance when it came to other religions and what the practices and iconography actually represented.

Ironically, Jesus never explicitly intended to start a new religion. His life was about deepening the spiritual understanding of his time, building on what came before, and emphasizing love and humility over strict adherence to rules. He added to the existing spirituality, not eradicating it, because love was his way. Similarly, Muhammad revered Jesus and added to his teachings, just as the Buddha enriched the spiritual history of the Indus Valley and its Hindu traditions. Throughout history, true religious teachers have been bridges between people and faiths, not barriers to unity. One cannot love Jesus and hate Muhammad or the Buddha, as they shared the same message and would have been allies in their missions on earth.

The Divine Unity

Believing one ideology to be the only truth and rejecting all others misses the point because an ideology is something that is "believed" and not necessarily lived. Ideology attempts to point to truth, but it is not the truth itself. We can think of religion as more like a road sign pointing in a certain direction. The direction is not the destination. Religion suggests an inner spiritual journey, which is separate from external affiliation with groups and customs.

Those who adhere strictly to dogma often become overly fixated on belonging, proving their righteousness, and earning their place in heaven. They think in terms of us and them, good and evil. This polarized thinking causes them to view the world in absolutes, missing the broader, more nuanced reality. Transcending this dualistic, black-and-white thinking about which religion is right, who is saved, and who is damned, is what all spiritual traditions originally aimed to impart. This transcendence is rooted in the practice of awareness—seeing things just as they are, without judgment.

I've met people from different religious backgrounds who insist their beliefs are the only right ones. Some Jews still view themselves as the chosen ones; some Christians believe Jesus is the only path to salvation, and some Muslims declare their faith as the ultimate form of God's message. People who make these claims display arrogance and ignorance, and in many ways, are engaging in a form of idolatry by worshiping their beliefs instead of the divine source. That is true sacrilege.

This type of dualistic thinking extends far beyond religion. We see it in nationalistic movements, when people will do anything, no matter how barbarous, for their country. At the moment, the fighting in Palestine and Israel is the worst it has been in a long time. Plenty of innocent people are being killed every day, and people are still engaged in debates about who is right and who is wrong, trying to explain how all these deaths are the result of some political decision made in the past. But imagine a world where people are not so focused on the divisions of us and them. There would be less killing and hate if we could simply recognize our shared humanity and put that first.

The Journey of Oneness

My deeper understanding of spirituality began when I was fifteen, during a trip to India with my aunt Layla, after whom my daughter is named. We visited the ashram of Sai Baba, a spiritual guru known for his teachings on unity, love, and service to humanity, and revered by millions around the world. Surrounded by people from various faiths at his ashram, I engaged in lively discussions with others, witnessed diverse spiritual practices, and experienced moments of deep spiritual connection. These experiences opened my eyes to a more nuanced understanding of spirituality—one that deeply resonated with my heart. The message was not about joining anything, but about eliminating the barriers between us, others, and the divine. It was not about separation or exclusivity, but about fostering oneness with everything.

It was on this first trip that I finally understood spirituality was about an inner path. Everything I had learned from religion started to make sense in a completely different context. I realized that true spirituality wasn't about choosing "right" or "wrong," but about embracing a journey of surrender and awareness. Awareness and surrender are deeply connected, like two sides of the same coin. Awareness requires surrendering our consciousness to the present moment, which will always be greater than ourselves. A higher power. I learned that choosing to cultivate this awareness is what it truly means to surrender to God. In awareness is where wisdom and compassion are found

My journey into Eastern religions influenced my spiritual outlook. I was drawn to the Vedic texts for their profound explanations of the universe. I learned about the importance of awareness in consciousness, the cycles of life, and the interconnectedness of all things. I embraced the teachings on non-attachment and compassion, for a gentler way of being, and began practicing meditation and chanting to cultivate peace and clarity in my mind.

Before my first trip to India, I'd been taught that monotheistic religions, which believe in one God, were the only rational option and that polytheistic beliefs were misguided, and that the idea of multiple deities was evil and wrong. Ironically, it was the polytheistic ideas of oneness that allowed me to truly understand what the monotheistic faiths were saying. Unfortunately, people get hung up on first impressions. Western religions might condemn polytheism, but they look quite similar if we take into account all the saints, apostles, angels and agents of God, not to mention a holy mother.

Despite rampant misconceptions, polytheistic religions also acknowledge a supreme divine entity, with multiple deities representing various facets of the one. They view nature as filled with spirit. In traditions like Buddhism, Hinduism, and many early human spiritualities, all of creation was held sacred. Mountains, rivers, and even our own bodies were revered because there was seen to be no divide between the creator and creation. The deities represented different aspects of this single divine source, emphasizing the interconnectedness of all things.

I'm not suggesting that all polytheists grasp unity. Some may indeed fall into superstition and nonsense, worshiping what appears to be merely an idol, as people in monotheistic faiths are sure to do as well. There are subgroups within every religion that misconstrue the message and start worshiping an ideal, an idea, or the religion itself instead of what those things point to—a multidimensional, omnipresent and singular God.

When we examine religions closely—whether it's the the ones most practiced today, or even more ancient religions like that of ancient Egypt—in their original contexts, a common thread emerges. Each religion, in its own way, says that God is within us and that everything is one. The three main monotheistic faiths—Christianity, Islam, and Judaism—account for over 60% of the world's population. Despite their influence, I find that the transcending of duality through awareness to uncover the divine presence within is not emphasized enough. Instead, the focus tends to be on dualistic concepts of sin and redemption, following strict rules, or accepting a savior or message as the absolute truth. This focus on absolutist ideas can overshadow the deeper teachings about the unity of all existence and the inner path.

The Essence of the Original Teachings

Followers often lose touch with the original languages and contexts of their scriptures, which can lead to misunderstandings of their religious texts. In the Arab world, the spread of Wahhabi ideals from the Arabian Peninsula has significantly influenced modern interpretations of Islam, often deviating from its original teachings and leading to extremist interpretations of scripture. Many readers of the Quran who are influenced by Wahhabism consider their interpretation of Islam as definitive, without exploring the historical and theological origins it shares with Judaism and Christianity. This broader understanding is necessary for a fuller interpretation of religion, but they are quick to say that all others are wrong instead of looking for commonality.

Likewise, many Christians and Jews are unfamiliar with Hebrew and Aramaic, the original languages of their scriptures, which causes them to miss nuanced aspects of what their faith says. Christianity underwent significant transformations as its epicenter shifted to Rome, and further changes occurred during the Crusades. As the political seat of Christianity moved to Europe, the religion was positioned in opposition to the Eastern world, particularly with the rise of the Islamic Ottoman Empire. This shift led to Christianity being viewed as a Western religion, distancing itself from its Eastern origins. As a result, some original teachings that require interpretation in their original Eastern context are widely misunderstood by Western practitioners. Over the centuries, the cultural rift has deepened, with Western Christianity often setting itself against what it perceives as its ideological enemies in the East. The Allah of Islam is a derivative of Elahi in Aramaic and Hebrew. I've heard many Christians refer to Allah as some type of foreign deity to them, unaware that their scriptures use essentially the same name for God.

Over the centuries, interpretations have deviated from the original intended meaning, but all religions aim to express the idea of oneness in their own ways. For example, Buddhists and Hindus speak about freeing oneself from *maya*, or illusion, to reach enlightenment. This journey to enlightenment involves moving beyond the everyday illusions of the senses to experience the deeper truth that everything is one.

The concept of oneness is deeply explored in Judaism through Kabbalah, which describes the universe as emanating from "Ein Sof," the infinite nature of God. According to Kabbalah, everything in the universe is derived from this divine source. This idea of oneness is also embodied in the Shema, a central prayer and verse from Deuteronomy that says, "Hear, O Israel: The Lord our God, the Lord is One," emphasizing that there is one God who is the singular divine essence of all existence.

Similarly, in Islam, the principle of Tawhid—the absolute oneness of God—is vividly articulated through the Quranic verse "Qul huwa Allahu ahad," meaning, "Say, He is Allah, who is One." This central tenet underpins not only the monotheistic faith itself but also enriches its spiritual practices and artistic expressions. Sufism, the mystical branch of Islam, embraces this unity through practices like meditation, dance, and chanting, aiming to dissolve the ego and achieve spiritual oneness with the divine. The intricate geometric patterns in Islamic art also reflect this principle, symbolizing infinite repetition and the boundless nature of the Creator.

Christianity expresses the concept of oneness through the idea of the Body of Christ, where believers are seen as parts of a single spiritual entity. Jesus's teachings emphasize oneness through his calls for self-denial, humility, unconditional love, and forgiveness. His message underscores transcending duality through awareness, achieved by surrendering to God and living fully in the present moment, free from attachment. Jesus's command to love your enemies transcends the duality of good people and bad people, showing that love and compassion are universal principles. His miraculous life also served as one of the most powerful examples in human history of the divine being accessible through an inner path of devotion. He wasn't saying, "I'm the only one," but rather, "We are all one," and "I am the proof."

All religions preach abandonment of the self for acceptance of the one and prescribe many practices to cultivate this sense of surrender. Charity, fasting, practicing awareness, and loving our enemies are forms of surrender. An emptying of self. That emptiness of self leaves room for something greater to come in. Jesus illustrates this with the metaphor of a camel passing through the eye of a needle.

"Again, I tell you, it is easier for a camel to go through the eye of a needle than for a rich person to enter the kingdom of God."

While some think he's talking about how difficult it is for a rich person to enter the kingdom of God, what he's really saying here is that overcoming mental and material attachment is the path to spiritual enlightenment. Just as it is physically impossible for a camel to pass through such a small opening, it is equally challenging for those attached to their own psychological structures to experience the unity of creation. There must be non-attachment and surrender.

Recognizing the Creator in the Creation

When we practice awareness, we discover that the same life force that animates us is present throughout all of creation. This realization reduces worries about what to believe, which religion to join, or how many gods there might be. We come to understand that there is just one reality—the creator and the creation are one.

In the spread of Christianity and Islam, despite their original messages of peace, there was much violence and division, driven by political agendas, fostering an us-versus-them mentality. These religions often clashed with different faiths and traditions of the time, some of which were polytheistic and revered nature. Monotheistic zealots, seeking to establish their "one true path," labeled these nature-worshipping cultures as pagans and devil worshippers. Defining themselves in opposition, they stripped the divine from the natural world, deeming reverence for nature as blasphemy. As a result, many Christians and Muslims today do not communicate the idea that the creation and the creator are one. Instead, God lives in a heaven far removed from the toils and wretched sins of humanity.

One of the biggest mistakes in modern religion, driven by dualistic thinking, is placing God in a distant heaven and removing Him from nature. This shift has made Earth a place of suffering and heaven a place to attain, leading to a disconnection with the world. From this perspective, it is easy to misunderstand and judge those who see the sacred in nature, dismissing them as pagans. Such judgment lies at the heart of many religious conflicts.

In truth, it's not about worshiping either the creator or the creation, but both. Reality is multidimensional. Just as my home is more than just walls, doors, wood, and bricks, our understanding of God must go beyond a singular interpretation. True spiritual surrender involves embracing the paradoxes that transcend duality. There is much more to experience in this life than mere religious affiliation.

4. Integrating Body, Mind, and Soul

Practicing awareness is essential for uncovering the truth of who we are and fully embracing our humanity, but it shouldn't be approached with an absolutist mindset. It would be ironic if I wrote this book for my daughter, telling her to avoid black-and-white thinking, and then boldly declared that my way was the only way. As Obi-Wan famously told Darth Vader in *Star Wars, Episode 3*, "Only a Sith deals in absolutes."

Being present in the moment requires awareness of the body. A person is considered meditative when their mind is clear, and they are present to the sensations in their body, instead of wandering with their thoughts. In these states of awareness, the spiritual nature of reality starts to become apparent.

Sometimes, our psychological processes can make us feel isolated. We experience life as distinct beings, separate from one another, but the truth is we are connected with each other and with the divine. This is because the creator and the creation are one and the same, and we exist within the creation. While we are individual beings, we are also part of a deeper reality; some would call it a life force that interconnects everything in the universe.

I don't think much about my daughter's future SAT scores at the moment (she's five), but I do think about sharing this valuable lesson with her, that when we learn to integrate body, mind, and soul through the practice of awareness, we awaken to the deeper reality. We experience ourselves as a trinity of body, mind, and soul.

Beyond Physical and Mental Boundaries

As human beings, we have complex minds and bodies and the freedom to shape our own lives. This ability is both a blessing and a curse. Unlike a dog, who doesn't ask existential questions, we can overthink to the point of harming ourselves. We have the most sophisticated brains on the planet, but they need careful management to prevent slipping into obsessiveness, fantasy, or misery. Similarly, our bodies are remarkable machines that need to be exercised and fully engaged to perform at their best.

By regularly meditating, we can significantly enhance every aspect of our lives. Managing our minds more effectively allows us to respond to life's challenges with greater calmness and clarity, rather than reacting impulsively. This heightened awareness also improves our connection to our bodies. The calmer our minds, the more sensitive we become to our bodies' needs and signals, intuitively reaching for the things that benefit our health, instead of harm it. The simple practice of awareness can help prevent overeating, reduce lethargy, improve posture, combat depression, stop addictive behaviors, and add a profound sense of meaning and purpose to one's life.

When we cultivate awareness in our body and mind, practicing being fully present, something remarkable happens—we begin to experience that we are more than just our physical form and our thoughts. We begin to connect with our soul. This awakening to a spiritual dimension within shows us the true essence of what we are.

There was a period in my mid-thirties when I felt completely disconnected from my body and mind. I was trying to build a sales team that wasn't succeeding, and unexpectedly, my business partner left. I had poured so much of my energy into achieving success and attached so much of my self-worth to the outcome of this venture that when the setbacks came, I was left spinning in mental anguish. I was caught in a relentless cycle of compulsive thoughts and behaviors, often overeating despite my best intentions and struggling constantly with negative thoughts. This time was incredibly frustrating as I felt increasingly out of control and disconnected from myself. Despite being health-oriented, I gained a significant amount of weight, and I developed sleep apnea.

Desperate for a change, I did something out of the box. I went to a spiritual retreat and took psychedelic compounds prepared by a guide, or shaman, in a group setting. I knew these types of ceremonies could be very healing, and that was my experience. Someone described it as "ten years of therapy in a single night," and the way I changed afterwards suggests its true.

Immediately after this experience, I revisited a meditation practice I had abandoned years before. This time, I approached it with renewed seriousness and sincerity, marking a significant turning point in my life. I started meditating every day and the inner discipline was there. Months later, I saw the noticeable distance I had created between my mind and my body. I began to see my "self" as the consciousness observing my thoughts and controlling my body, which were possessions of mine, but not "me." This small shift in perspective from meditation allowed me to observe my thoughts and reactions from a more detached perspective, instead of getting immediately caught up in them. As a result, I gained much better control over my mental and emotional processes.

After making these changes, my mind became calmer, and my eating habits improved as I naturally started choosing whole foods, fruits, and vegetables. The pounds just started falling off, and my sleep apnea disappeared. I also began practicing yoga, which seemed to happen naturally. While I had always prioritized exercise, I found myself newly interested in the idea of flexibility, dedicating myself to improving my posture, opening my hips, and increasing mobility. I began to move my body with more confidence, awareness, and gratitude throughout my daily life.

Amazingly, practicing awareness allowed me to achieve much more at work than I had accomplished before. Everything seemed to flow without the need to grind gears. Business relationships formed naturally, and I was able to put good deals together. These deals were more lucrative and fun to work on than the things I had been working on before.

Society and our natural conditioning sometimes make us experience life as if we are just our bodies or just our minds. We identify each other by physical characteristics, and we place a high value on intelligence and the ability to retain information. We also give immense power to the idea that we have unique personalities and that our preferences make us who we are. However, the reality is that change is the only constant, and it is only by being aware of and present to these changes that we discover who we really are.

Achieving Inner and Outer Harmony

I stumbled across this unattributed quote on social media, and it made me stop.

"If you feel like you hate everybody, eat something. If you feel like everybody hates you, go to sleep. If you feel like you hate yourself, have a shower. If you feel like everyone hates everyone, go outside."

As simple as this wisdom is, it clearly points to how our actions affect our state of mind, and how we suffer when we're not aware. It is common for many of us to get overwhelmed by our thoughts and feelings, yet often the solution can be as simple as eating healthy, going outside, or talking to a friend. Living too much in the mind and out of the body is one of the greatest causes of suffering in the world.

When I explain this to my daughter, I'll make it simple. I'll tell her to imagine that tomorrow she'll have the most important meeting of her life—a one-on one chat with God.

Then I would ask her a series of questions. How will you prepare for it? What would you eat beforehand? Will you show up showered and well dressed? If you needed to, would you spend some time outside, walking and clearing your head before the meeting?

The point I'm making that I hope comes across clearly is how we show up to every moment matters, because the truth is, we are never not sitting with God. But to extend the analogy further, if I could actually sit with and talk to God directly, I'd want to present the best version of myself. This would go beyond just taking a shower and dressing nicely. Beforehand, I'd choose to eat something light and nourishing, like fruits or vegetables, to ensure my mind stays clear and focused. During the meeting, assuming I wasn't blinded by the light, I'd make sure to sit up straight, look directly ahead, and show utmost respect.

Now, imagine instead that I had eaten a lot of Taco Bell before the appointment, causing my stomach to rumble during our time together. Or maybe I had consumed a bag of gummy bears, and some alcohol, so that I was jittery and drunk. Sitting there unshowered and unclean, mentally distracted, and slouching in the seat across from God, I wonder why meeting him wasn't as amazing as I thought it would be. The irony is obvious, and the point is, how we treat ourselves matters. Our posture, what we put in our bodies, and our inner attitude all matter in our experience of life and in spirituality.

I want to reiterate this point that we are always in the presence of God because the creation and the creator are one. Therefore, how we hold ourselves, how we carry ourselves, breathe, eat, and speak, all directly impact our experience of the divine. I've been the person who opts for fast food, has poor sleep, slouches, and spends all day in front of screens, wondering why I don't feel spiritually connected. This is a common experience for many, but the truth is hiding in plain sight.

As straightforward as it might sound, lots of people do not see the connection between their physical well-being and their spiritual experiences. They go to temples, mosques, or churches to listen to ideology and learn about God, but they don't understand that every gesture, every bite of food, every word spoken, if intentional, is an experience of the divine.

The Trinity of Body, Mind, and Soul

In many traditions, spiritual practices are designed to help individuals achieve internal coherence. In the yogic tradition, practitioners use specific poses to move their energy in certain ways, clearing their minds in preparation for meditation. This alignment of body and mind creates a state conducive to deeper spiritual awareness. Yoga, which means "union" in Sanskrit, refers to the integration of the self with the greater universe through physical and mental coherence.

Other religions and disciplines also have practices aimed at developing internal coherence, though they look very different across cultures. Nonetheless, across the board, there are some commonalities. The most spiritually attuned people I know maintain good posture, eat fresh foods, uphold cleanliness, are kind to others, and their consciousness is deeply focused yet relaxed. They engage in spiritual practices like prayer, meditation, chanting, singing, dance, nature walks, and breathing exercises, to quiet the mind and create alignment.

Practices like yoga or prostrating in prayer are not merely symbolic—they are exercises in geometry, aligning and shaping our bodies in ways that enhance our physical and spiritual presence. Maintaining a straight back instead of slouching can significantly improve both our everyday demeanor in life and our health. Similarly, the positions assumed during meditation, prayer, and yoga—like the folding of legs and opening of hands—each serve a specific function in connecting us with the inner reality.

When I was younger, I hated being told to sit up straight. I was a sloucher, and it seemed like such a trivial thing. But as an adult, I've come to appreciate the importance of good posture and have incorporated it into more than just the way I sit. It's become a guiding principle in every aspect of my life. I kneel to express humility. I bring my hands together in gratitude. I try to align my words with my actions. I chant, pray, meditate, practice yoga, and give to others—not because religion suggests it, but because every moment, every gesture, matters.

Many activities that foster internal coherence, such as meditation or yoga, require minimal intellectual effort. This is important because, while the mind is an essential part of our existence, it is not all that we are. Some scientists reduce all human experiences to mere electrical impulses in the brain, a view that is overly simplistic and blind to the larger reality. The full experience of being human extends beyond the mind. Our bodies respond to love—our hearts beat faster, our pupils dilate, our emotions soar. We experience rushes of energy. We love with our whole beings, not through intellectual deduction. The love I have for my daughter is infinite, and it is not because of something I figured out in my mind. It's spiritual as much as it is biological.

Connecting With All of Creation

Everything originated from the Big Bang, an explosion of a massive star. This explosion gave birth to our universe, including our planet and, ultimately, our bodies because the atoms from that star eventually became everything that we know. We are made up of stardust, standing on a planet also made of stardust, revolving around the sun, which is another star born of that first ancient star. We rely on nutrients from plants that convert the sun's energy through photosynthesis and interact with a world that is only visible because of the sun's light. We consist of the same stuff as everything else.

The unification of body, mind, and soul through awareness deepens our understanding of the world and our place in it. When we cultivate this awareness, somehow, we begin to see from experience how our atoms are the same as all other atoms in the universe. We feel a connection to the millions of years of evolution it took for us to exist in our sophisticated human bodies. We intuitively understand that our bodies were once part of the stars, just as our souls are part of the same creative intelligence that made everything we know.

The food we consume becomes part of our bodies, and upon our death, it all returns to the soil, providing sustenance for other life forms. Within us, countless microorganisms thrive, outnumbering the cells we typically recognize as "ours." In this vast ecosystem that is our planet, we are merely a small part, yet to the microorganisms within us, we represent an entire universe. As odd as it may seem, when we practice awareness and develop inner coherence, these concepts transform from abstract ideas into tangible experiences. We begin to feel the profound interconnectedness of life, and how each of us comes from something much more ancient than our minds could comprehend.

I've found that the more I achieve inner coherence, the more attuned I become to the natural world around me, including the weather, seasons, elements, and distant planets. Our ancestors recognized this connection for thousands of years. They observed how the moon's phases affected not only ocean tides but also their emotions. They constructed elaborate temples to embody this concept of coherence, aligning with cardinal directions and astronomical events like solstices and equinoxes. From these ancient remnants, we can see that our ancestors understood the vital bond tying our beings to the greater rhythms of the universe.

Today, it's all too common for people to live disconnected from their bodies and the greater world. The comforts of modern life have drawn us indoors, distancing us from the natural cycles and, ironically, from our own bodies. But when we find inner coherence and awareness, we realize our soul is the universe itself. If I can help my daughter experience this, I'll have done my job as a father.

5. Ancient Wisdom and Modern Insights

As an Egyptian, I appreciate that western history books connect the time of the pharaohs with the birth of human civilization on earth, but I hope to teach my daughter a broader and more realistic perspective. It's crucial to consider the history of humanity without judgment or ideological arrogance. Modern historical narratives often say that human civilization began relatively recently, citing ancient societies like Sumer around 4000 BC and ancient Egypt around 3100 BC as examples. However, there's another story to consider—one that suggests human civilization is much older and more complex than mainstream history indicates.

While it's tempting to see our era as the peak of human development, I also suggest a different perspective here. We ought to view the past as a different expression of the same humanity, instead of a more primitive version of us. Our ancestors faced different challenges than we do today, and we face different challenges than they did. Understanding where we came from is crucial for knowing where we are heading, and to do that, we must see things for what they are, each era in its own context.

The Depth of Ancient Civilizations

I've always been fascinated by ancient history. It wasn't until later in life that I realized just how far back that history stretches. Egyptologists typically trace ancient Egypt's origins to around 5,000 years ago, about 500 years before the proposed construction date of the pyramids. However, growing evidence, first brought forward and entertained by fringe scientists and investigators, suggests that Egypt's history may go back much further. These alternative perspectives are now gaining traction in mainstream academia, and it's likely that new dates will soon be widely accepted as part of our shared human history. The textbooks will have to be rewritten.

The Great Sphinx of Giza is one of the most intriguing pieces of evidence. Geologist Robert Schoch has argued that the clear signs of water erosion, especially visible around its enclosure, suggest the Sphinx was exposed to heavy rainfall sometime in its existence. This suggests that the Sphinx might have been carved during a period with a wetter climate, challenging the commonly accepted construction date of 2500 BCE and suggesting a much earlier origin, potentially thousands of years earlier. The erosion patterns on the Sphinx suggest that the necessary climate for such erosion existed over 12,000 years ago, predating the region's transformation into the arid Sahara Desert, indicating a time when the area was lush and habitable.

This view challenges the conventional timeline for the emergence of advanced civilization and monumental architecture in Egypt. It suggests that civilization existed before the Younger Dryas events, which occurred approximately 12,900 to 11,700 years ago and were marked by abrupt climatic shifts. Scholars note that flood narratives found in ancient texts such as the Old Testament, Quran, Mayan history, and Zoroastrian history may allude to these significant cataclysmic events that occurred during these earlier periods in Earth's history.

When we examine the astronomical alignments of the Sphinx and pyramids of Giza, we find they correspond to specific stars in the ancient sky. The same is true of Mesoamerican pyramids, mounds, and petroglyphs, as well as a number of ancient structures in Anatolia. The pyramids align with the three belt stars of Orion, the Tomb of the Birds, an often-overlooked structure on the Giza plateau, aligns with the constellation Cygnus, and the Great Sphinx points at the constellation Leo. These alignments are precise in terms of geometric angles and degrees. However, they do not correspond to the time when scientists say these monuments were built but to a picture of the night sky around 10,500 BCE, according to researcher Graham Hancock.

Another intriguing artifact and piece of evidence for an earlier origin date for human civilization is the Abydos King List. Housed in the temple of Seti I at Abydos, this list chronicles a succession of pharaohs back to a time when "gods" walked the earth. Similarly, the Sumerian King List, an ancient manuscript discovered in Mesopotamia and recorded in the Sumerian language, traces a lineage of god-kings with reigns spanning thousands of years. The Sumerian King List includes rulers who reigned before a Great Flood. These timelines predate the commonly accepted beginnings of recorded history and suggest a much older origin for human civilization. The ancients didn't carve megalithic stones or spend years inscribing these messages without reason. Their efforts imply a deep significance and should not be dismissed, despite how fantastical the history seems.

The theme of a lost ancient era resonates across various cultural narratives. Abrahamic texts recount figures like Noah and Abraham interacting with giants and facing global floods. Hindu scriptures detail cycles of yugas, suggesting advanced civilizations tens of thousands of years ago. Aboriginal Australian narratives align with geological findings of submerged land bridges and coastal changes from before the last Ice Age. The Mayan and Zoroastrian texts also contribute to the global memory of catastrophic floods.

These interconnected myths hint at forgotten eras in human history. Our ancestors built incredible monuments that remind us of their rich legacy. Just as it's hard for us to truly conceptualize that dinosaurs once roamed the earth and that early hominid species thrived for millions of years, our ancestors may have seen and done things beyond our current understanding. While we marvel at our own accomplishments, we are equally astonished by the feats of the ancients. Let us not judge the past by the standards of the present.

Exploring More Ancient Origins

Evidence from various parts of the world challenges the conventional timeline of human civilization as recognized by mainstream academia. Göbekli Tepe in Turkey stands out as a significant example, dated to around 9600 BC, using radiocarbon dating techniques. This site features megalithic pillars with precise astronomical alignments, suggesting advanced masonry skills and organized labor systems far earlier than previously thought. It predates the supposed construction date of the pyramids by more than 6,000 years.

Similarly, the town of Baalbek in Lebanon houses massive stone blocks that some scholars think are much older than the Roman structures built there. Some theories suggest that these ancient stones, known as the trilithon, might be over 9,000 years old.

In Indonesia, the megalithic site of Gunung Padang challenges conventional timelines, with radiocarbon dating suggesting ages surpassing 20,000 years. The site's terraces and large stone columns indicate advanced engineering skills that could push the history of human settlement in the region much further back than previously thought.

Recent research is prompting a reevaluation of the age and origins of many ancient sites around the world. Easter Island, known for its moai statues, traditionally dated to 1100–1500 CE, now suggests a much older cultural heritage. Stonehenge's initial constructions date back to at least 3000–2920 BC. The megalithic walls in Peru's Sacsayhuamán, part of a larger complex near Cusco, showcase advanced engineering techniques and are thought to be much older than previously believed. Similarly, Malta's Ġgantija Temples, among the world's oldest free-standing structures, built with massive megaliths that boggle the mind, are now being reconsidered as potentially much older.

What we consider ancient might actually be quite recent in the timeline of human history. For perspective, the Hindu Vedas were composed around 7,000 years ago, followed by the foundation of Judaism about 3,000 years ago. Buddhism emerged 2,600 years ago, Jesus Christ lived around 2,000 years ago, and Prophet Muhammad founded Islam only 1,400 years ago.

A reimagined timeline of human civilization is needed and might put some of our mythologies into context. As Plato wrote, approximately 12,000 years ago, Atlantis, an advanced island civilization in the Atlantic Ocean beyond the Straits of Gibraltar, sank under the waves in a global flood. Perhaps we should start to see this as history instead of fiction, and there are many scientists and historians alike who would now be confident enough to agree publicly.

Oneness in Ancient Cultures

Human progress isn't solely about modernity, technology, or cities. It should really be measured in degrees of awareness. Viewing humanity's history in cycles, where we move closer to or further from understanding ourselves, offers a more holistic perspective on the human story. In ancient times, people achieved remarkable levels of coherence within themselves and with nature. By expanding their consciousness, they were able to create megalithic wonders that mirrored the constellations above and continue to challenge our understanding of what our ancestors were capable of.

Rather than viewing our ancestors as primitive, compared to our current level of technological sophistication, we should shift our lens towards one of spirituality. If we look at our modern technology and advancements holistically, we see that they have often harmed the environment in order to provide us with comfort and convenience. This is not true progress. Let's instead evaluate societies by their understanding of interconnectedness, their impact on the planet, and the cultural norms that will influence future generations.

Studies in world religions and ancient mythologies reveal a consistent theme—throughout history, there have been times pockets of people who were profoundly aware of the truths I'm writing about in this book and intending to share with my daughter. We have evidence all over the world that, at times, our ancient ancestors were aware of the interconnectedness of all things, and that there was an inner path to experience the divine on earth. This recurring insight across different cultures points to one ultimate reality, regardless of religious origin or geographic location.

Ancient cultures are often misunderstood as simply worshiping many gods or revering animals and rocks, but this view is both arrogant and incorrect. The reason that modern people get tripped up and assume the ancients were animal worshipers is because of their iconography. In Egyptian mythology, deities like Amun-Ra and Horus represented different aspects of the self. Amun-Ra symbolized the human side, while Horus, often depicted as a falcon, symbolized the divine perspective from above. The ancients combined these two deities to communicate the idea of multidimensionality, and how we were capable of connecting with a greater reality by turning inward.

Deities like Isis, Hathor, and Nephthys represented different facets of the human-divine connection. Together, these female deities illustrated what it meant to embody feminine energy. They were seen as aspects of a single deity. Isis was the creator, Hathor the sustainer of life and giver of milk, and Nephthys the force of destruction. The ancients viewed the creative spark that gave rise to everything as masculine, while the world itself was perceived as feminine; a concept echoed in many cultures. We see similar ideas in Hinduism, where the goddess Kali represents creation, preservation, and destruction—inevitable forces in the world.

For millennia, humanity lived in closer harmony with nature, under the open stars, which reinforced the experience that everything is interconnected. In the time before books and the internet, people conveyed ideas using symbols they were familiar with. Thus, using a cow, a provider of milk, to represent the feminine aspect of humanity made perfect sense in their context. Today, many of us have forgotten what it means to live in harmony with nature, but the patterns that the ancients recognized are the same patterns present in our reality.

The Sophistication of Ancient Technology

Our history is not merely a linear progression toward technological sophistication, as modern society suggests. The ancients had access to knowledge and abilities we still do not fully understand. The Pyramids of Giza serve as remarkable examples of ancient technology, showcasing not just architectural brilliance but also profound connections to astronomical, mathematical, and metaphysical insights.

One fascinating aspect of these pyramids is their alignment with Orion's Belt. The positioning of the three pyramids—Khufu, Khafre, and Menkaure—mirrors the arrangement of the three stars in Orion's Belt when observed from a specific viewpoint on the ground with shocking precision.

In terms of measurements, the dimensions of the Great Pyramid are thought to contain detailed knowledge about the Earth. For example, the height of the Great Pyramid multiplied by 43,200 equals the polar radius of the Earth, suggesting a deliberate incorporation of Earth's dimensions into its design. In addition, the pyramid's dimensions hold key mathematical principles, with its perimeter-to-height ratio coming out very close to the figure for π (pi). The golden ratio is reflected in it, and the geographic coordinates of the Great Pyramid of Giza (29.9792458° N) also closely resemble the speed of light in meters per second.

The Great Pyramid is also known for its remarkable sound properties, particularly in the King's Chamber, where sound resonates in a manner that could enhance meditation and induce altered states of consciousness. Acoustic researcher John Stuart Reid has studied these effects, suggesting that the ancient builders designed these places not just as feats of engineering, but for spiritual enlightenment through sound manipulation. I have meditated in and near the Great Pyramid, and it indeed has a powerful effect on consciousness. It's an incredible thing that I will share with my daughter when she's old enough to understand.

We see similarly impressive ancient ingenuity at sites around the world, such as Machu Picchu and Easter Island, where massive stones are arranged in ways that suggest almost otherworldly skill. At Machu Picchu, located in the Andes Mountains of Peru, the structures are expertly crafted with stones so precisely cut that they fit together without the need for mortar. Meanwhile, on Easter Island, the iconic moai statues—enormous monoliths carved from volcanic rock—are meticulously aligned, raising questions about the methods used by the island's inhabitants to create and move them. All structures also have astrological alignments, further complicating matters.

The ancients constructed monuments with a precision that today's technology struggles to replicate. Our time is defined by technologies like radio, television, and the internet, but in many ways, our technology is just a new iteration of what was attempted before. The internet serves to disseminate information globally and elevate collective consciousness, just as the pyramids were meant to do, raising people's awareness through mathematics, astronomy, acoustics, and the practice of meditation.

Understanding Sacred Languages

It's not often thought of this way, but language is a technology. One of the most valuable advancements passed down by our ancestors is language. Arabic, Aramaic, Hebrew, Sanskrit, and Greek are more than just means of communication; they are repositories of ancient wisdom, each syllable resonating with significance. Many cultures believe these languages to be divinely inspired, gifted to humanity to aid in a deeper understanding of the cosmos and our place in it.

As an author, I deeply appreciate the English language for its versatility and vast vocabulary. However, it often lacks the words for certain types of wisdom found in ancient languages, making it less effective for describing spiritual experience and the essence of oneness. English is an object-specific language, where each object has its own distinct term, often without connections to related concepts. For example, the word "love" refers specifically to an emotion, without inherently connecting to other related concepts like "heart" or "soul."

In contrast, ancient languages are more interconnected. In Arabic, for example, the word for love (hubb) shares a root with the word for seed (habb), suggesting that love is the seed from which all things grow. In Hebrew, the word for man (adam) is directly linked to the word for earth (adamah), emphasizing the relationship between humans and the earth. These connections in ancient languages are very complex and allow for a richer and more holistic understanding of life.

Just as Sanskrit is fundamental to Hindu spiritual practices, the Abrahamic faiths are deeply rooted in their languages. Hebrew, Arabic, and Aramaic are very connected with each other as well as internally and steeped in spirituality. They are context-specific as opposed to object-specific, with combinations of words evolving together over time to reflect profound insights into spiritual and existential realms. For example, in Aramaic, (napsha) is the word for "self," while (nafas) signifies "breath," suggesting an inherent link between breath and self-awareness. In meditation, focusing on the breath helps set the mind aside. Similarly, accessing one's soul (ruha) is the key to discovering inner peace (rahma).

Looking at Jesus's words in their original Aramaic can guide followers toward a more profound understanding of his teachings, particularly on the concept of oneness. In Aramaic, he never claimed to be God's only son in the exclusive sense often interpreted. The word he used for "son" (*bar*) can also mean "grain," or "seed,." What he was really expressing was how everything and everyone is part of God. This interpretation emphasizes unity rather than exclusivity. He wasn't saying he is the only example of divinity, and all other paths are wrong. When Jesus said, "I am the way, the truth, and the life," he was pointing to himself as an example of the potential for achieving oneness with the creator. But in theological interpretations, those who cling to ideological differences will argue that he was saying, "me and no one else."

Exploring the beatitudes in Aramaic paints a different picture of Jesus's message, because he spoke Aramaic, not Greek, and it is within the cultural context of his language that the full meaning of his words can be understood.

When he said, "Blessed are those who are poor in spirit; the kingdom of heaven belongs to them," he was speaking about awareness. The word (tubyayun) in Aramaic, typically translated as "blessed," also means "ripe," as in the ripeness of a fruit. This is significant because the world comes from the root word (tub), meaning "center." This suggests that being "ripe" involves being in balance and transcending the dualities of past and future, good and bad. Another interpretation of this beatitude is that those who are "empty" in spirit, and practice non-attachment, are blessed and will have access to the divine.

Words and names matter. I've always found it odd that when someone walks into a yoga studio, they have no problem saying namaste to greet others, and no problem saying the Sanskrit names of the poses they are performing. But when it comes to Western Christianity, adherents of the faith refuse to use the real names.

In Aramaic, Jesus's name is Esho, which means "life." This is the name his mother, Mariam, gave him—a name rich with profound meaning. Mariam, often translated as "Mary," holds the equally profound meaning of "bitter beloved," which beautifully reflects the sacrifices she and her son made. I believe saying their real names has power and connects us to them in a way that transcends sermons and ideology.

The names of archangels in the original Hebrew also hold significant meaning and collectively point to the idea of oneness. All angel names denote ownership by God. Gabriel means the "might of God," Michael means "who is like God," and Nuriel means "the light of God." Samael, the fallen angel who is often misunderstood, means "the poison of God." Though it is hard for people who approach religion with black and white thinking and polarize the message into good and bad to understand this, Samael's name doesn't denote evil. Rather, his role is one aspect of God's creation—the darkness that makes the light shine brighter. He serves a purpose in the divine plan and is therefore part of the greater whole, because God isn't just one. Everything is one.

We see sophisticated languages in other ancient traditions as well. In Hinduism, which draws deeply from the Sanskrit Vedas, the vocabulary for understanding of the self and the mind is remarkably sophisticated. Sanskrit, the language of these ancient texts, allows for a highly nuanced exploration of consciousness. Similarly, Buddhist texts are also in Sanskrit and filled with concepts, verses, and mantras that emphasize the transcendence over duality to achieve enlightenment.

6. The Fabric of Reality

As I've grown more introspective and committed to my meditation practice, spending quiet moments with my eyes closed and focusing on being fully present, I've noticed a significant change in how I experience the world. This inward journey paradoxically deepens my connection to the universe. The stars, planets, and even the smallest particles like atoms, protons, and electrons, which once seemed distant and abstract, now feel closer and more a part of my personal experience. There's a reason for this.

Paradoxes of Existence

When exploring the cosmos and our place within it, it's essential to embrace a universe-centric view rather than a human-centric one. Thinking of humanity as the main character in the universe's story is arrogant. The universe is believed to be around 13.8 billion years old. From a universe-centric view, we are not as important as we think we are

There are vastly more stars in the universe than there are people. With approximately two trillion galaxies in the observable universe, each containing around 100 billion stars, there are sextillions of stars—far exceeding the number of humans. If God created everything, we are but a minuscule part of the plan. By adopting a broader perspective, we begin to take on a humbler approach when drawing conclusions about what we are, recognizing the vastness and mystery of the universe.

There is a profound paradox in our experience of the universe—we are both a part of it and live within it. This dual understanding is beautifully illustrated in the metaphor of Indra's net from Hindu and Buddhist philosophy. According to the Rig Veda, Indra's net is a vast, infinite web stretching across the universe. In each eye of the net, there is a radiant jewel that reflects every other jewel. One can look into one jewel and see all the others. The net symbolizes the interconnectedness of all things.

Another way of looking at it is that the universe itself is the body of God. The earth and the stars function like organs in this vast body, each serving a purpose for the greater whole. We, as individuals, are like cells within these organs. When we look deeply into one cell, we see the entirety because it is all part of a single being. This idea may seem paradoxical and hard to grasp intellectually, but through meditation and spiritual practices, this abstract concept can become a deeply personal experience.

The oneness perspective implies that everything in the universe carries divine spirit. This invites us to view the cosmos as an expression of the divine and challenges many traditional religious teachings that often view the divine as distinctly separate from the physical realm. By recognizing the universe as both the tangible physical reality and the divine presence, we can begin to grasp the concept of oneness through our own experiences.

I wish to teach my daughter that creation is sacred, and to live in a way that relates to the world around her. I wish for her to enjoy spending time in nature and appreciate the cycles of seasons and the movement of the stars. I want her to understand that knowing herself is an exercise in knowing the entire universe.

God is the Universal Mind

One of the most compelling stories about how the universe came to be is the creation narrative in the Rig Veda. It portrays a state of existence before creation, where neither existence nor non-existence prevailed. This primordial state isn't characterized by the absence of God but rather by a unified potentiality—an inherent divine potential waiting to unfold. From this void, a desire emerged as the initial spark of consciousness, setting in motion the process of creation.

Comparing this to the Old Testament, this moment in the Rig Veda aligns with when God contemplates. It echoes the biblical phrase "I am that I am," signifying self-awareness and existence. Subsequently, just as God commands "Let there be light" to initiate creation in the Bible, the Rig Veda portrays a desire that starts the formation of the universe, manifesting everything into the light and into existence.

In both Judaic and Vedic theologies, God is described as a consciousness or mind, and everything that exists is essentially an idea created by pure consciousness. We've talked about how consciousness affects matter, with subatomic particles acting as waves or matter, depending on whether they are being observed. In both quantum physics and religion, we find a clear connection regarding consciousness and matter. This is because one dimension of creation is pure consciousness, and we are constantly co-creating the world around us, though we are hardly aware of it.

The same idea has a reflection in Islam. The Quran venerates the spider as a holy creature because of how it weaves its web, symbolizing how we construct our realities. Just as the spider spins its web from substances it produces within, we shape our experiences through our thoughts and interactions with the universe. Unfortunately, for many people, it is only at the moment of death that they become aware of how they were actively shaping reality and everything within it.

Insights from individuals who have been resuscitated after clinical death, as well as from yogis in Eastern traditions who can significantly lower their heart rate to simulate the state of death in the body, often describe the world as an illusion, with no real division between "here" and "there." Death, therefore, is not so much a journey from one place to another but a transition from one form of consciousness to another.

The Universe Within Us

I can't reiterate enough that truth is paradoxical. The creator and the creation are one, but another paradox of reality is that each of us is like a universe unto ourselves. Many religions express that we are made in God's image. This doesn't imply that

God resembles a human but instead proclaims that we are creators of our reality. Consider anything we look at, whether it be a rainbow, a mountain, or a person—we are not really seeing them. Instead, we see light reflecting off these objects, entering our eyes, and being processed by our brain. This principle applies to all our senses, not just sight. Everything we experience is completely subjective to us and happens within us.

Touch isn't a direct interaction with an object, but a response triggered by pressure receptors in the skin. These receptors convert physical pressure into electrical signals that travel to the brain, creating the sensation of touch. Similarly, sound originates from air vibrations, which the ear translates into electrical signals for the brain to interpret as sound. When molecules enter the nose, they bind to receptors, sending signals to the brain that we interpret as different smells. Taste works similarly, where chemicals from food interact with taste receptors on the tongue. The point here is that, without exception, everything we experience happens within us.

Even our thoughts are internal phenomena. When you think of something, like a red ball, the mental image exists solely within your mind. If someone upsets us, the sadness doesn't exist in the world, but within us. All our thoughts and emotions occur within us. The world isn't happy or sad, but we create an emotional and intellectual landscape around it, shaping our individual realities.

We've never truly seen each other, the stars, or anything else directly. We've never touched anything external to us. In that way, every experience we have as humans exists solely within our own universes. The paradox is that there is a greater universe at work, too, and we are reflections of it. Each of us is a mirror to this vast cosmos, where every part and the whole are expressions of one. Even in looking at the stars, we only see ourselves.

Frequency and Vibration

Everything in the world is created through a dance between dualities. At the subatomic level, we see the vibrations of protons and electrons, positive and negative, manifesting the shapes we see.

Everything is vibrating, though we do not see it. The world is made of vibration, which is why some spiritual traditions say that creation is made of up sound. In religious practices, songs, chants, and spoken prayers are believed to connect us to the divine through the sounds themselves. These practices highlight the sacred nature of sound. The Hindu "Om" symbolizes the universe's birth from vibration, a primordial sound from which all things originate. Similarly, the Bible's phrase "let there be light" suggests that God's speech generates light.

In scientific terms, vibrations, or sound, play a crucial role in shaping creation. At its core, the universe operates as a symphony of vibrations. Sound only represents the vibrations that we can hear, the audible frequencies. When we hear sound, it's because vibrations travel through a medium, like air or water, and reach our ears. The frequency of these vibrations determines whether we perceive them as high or low pitch.

Human hearing typically ranges from about 20 to 20,000 Hertz, with frequencies below or above this range being inaudible to us.

The universe is also made of light, which is manifested by vibration. Sound and light, though different types of energy, share fascinating similarities in their wavelengths and frequencies. The frequency of a sound wave determines its pitch—higher frequencies produce higher pitches. Similarly, in light, frequency dictates color—higher frequencies result in blue or violet light, while lower frequencies produce red or orange. Both sound and light form spectra and can be reflected and refracted. Sound waves bounce back from hard surfaces and can be focused or dispersed, similar to how light reflects off mirrors or water. Refraction, when waves change direction, passing through different mediums, explains why a straw appears bent in water and why the sky looks blue.

White light contains the entire spectrum of colors. When it passes through a prism, it separates into a rainbow, each color with its distinct wavelength. This process illustrates how a single entity can become many. Similarly, sound frequencies can be separated and analyzed. In music, every melody is composed of notes from a scale, akin to how white light holds all the colors of the rainbow. The musical scale contains the potential for harmony and melody, just as light contains the colors.

Sound and Light in Spirituality and Healing

In all religious narratives, sound and light hold spiritual significance, even those religions that are no longer practiced or understood today. Ancient Egyptians honored light through the god Ra, who embodies the sun's essence as a symbol of life. There are many depictions of Amur Ra with the sun disk on his crown, using the light of the sun as a metaphor for enlightenment. The ancient Egyptians also used sound in their spirituality, as exemplified by the acoustic properties of the pyramids.

In Hinduism, "Om" is revered as the primordial sound of the cosmos. When it comes to meditation, light is often the focus of visualization. Christianity says, "In the beginning was the Word, and the Word was with God, and the Word was God," with "the Word" representing both the divine command that brought forth the universe and the being who commanded it. In the Bible, there are several references to God being pure light. The Aboriginals of Australia speak of ancestors from Dreamtime who sang the world into existence.

Science has shown that sound and light can have healing effects and real-world impacts. In the 1970s, researcher Dorothy Retallack conducted the Music and Plants Experiment, observing the effects of music on plant growth. She found that plants exposed to classical music thrived, growing towards the source of the sound and developing healthier leaves. In contrast, plants subjected to harsh, or rock, music showed signs of stress, growing away from the sound source and having stunted growth and withered leaves. When it comes to sharing music with my daughter, I'm sure I'll take her to a rock concert at least once, but I want her to be aware of the very real effect music could have on her, and to be mindful about what she listens to on a daily basis.

John Stuart Reid, a prominent English acoustics engineer, scientist, and inventor known for his extensive research in the field of cymatics, explored the effects of sound waves on physical materials. He developed an instrument that makes sound visible by imprinting sound vibrations onto water, revealing the geometric patterns that sound frequencies create. He also conducted an experiment, shown in *The Field* documentary, and dubbed the "concert for human blood." It demonstrated the impact of live music on human blood cells. During the experiment, music was played to a sample of human blood. The sound vibrations from the music caused the blood cells to become revitalized, exhibiting more vibrant and healthy movement. Conversely, playing dissonant noise killed the blood cells.

A different study by researchers at the University of Helsinki explored the effects of Gregorian chants on stress reduction. Participants listened to recordings of Gregorian chants daily for several weeks. The study measured stress levels using physiological markers, such as heart rate variability and cortisol levels. The results indicated that regular exposure to Gregorian chants significantly reduced stress levels among participants.

I recite Sanskrit mantras regularly, and they have transformed my life. I now think of our bodies as tuning forks, resonating with the vibrations around us. To experience the deeper reality, we need to tune our vibrations to higher frequencies, where both sound and light play a crucial role.

7. Who Am I?

Everything is a reflection of one. Every aspect of creation, from rocks and trees to you and me, is an expression of one perfect being. Despite appearing distinct, we are manifestations of a single, perfect existence, expressed in myriad forms. God is not merely the creator but also the creation, encompassing all entities within itself. Just as every drop of water is both part of the ocean and an ocean unto itself, we, too, are expressions of the same life-giving force that animates birds, wind, and trees. But if we are also distinct beings, then who are we really?

The fascinating paradox is that while we appear as separate entities, from a broader, non-human perspective, we are never actually ever apart from God. This dual perspective lets us experience oneness through both separation and union. It enables us to explore profound bonds of love with each other and all of creation, through both life and death. We enter this world unaware of our origins, but we are destined to rediscover them, dancing between polarities, until we find our true center.

One Expressed as Many

We belong to something greater than we can fully grasp with our finite human minds. But it is this truth that we must surrender to, submitting our identities and "selves" to a higher power. This surrender happens through awareness, not affiliation, and it allows us to experience firsthand our connection to the divine.

To surrender to God means recognizing that our innermost being transcends our physical form and the thoughts in our brains. Identifying solely with our bodies and personalities is limiting, as these aspects are not eternal. It might sound grim, but death is inevitable. Our bodies will eventually cease to function, and over time, even the memories others hold of us will fade. To declare anything within our transient experiences as absolute inevitably leads to contradictions. If I say that I am this or that, the statement can only hold true for so long.

If God exists within every person, creature, and object on this planet, why would such a powerful being choose to manifest in so many varied forms? To answer this question, we need to consider the nature of our lives on Earth and contrast them with an imagined perfect existence—what many would envision as heaven. This comparison between human and divine expectations can help shed light on the reason for God's diverse expressions—the reason behind it all.

Imagine a place where happiness never ends, where we're always with our loved ones, and there's no pain, loss, or death. At first, this might sound ideal, but imagine that this goes on for thousands or even millions of years. Without the ups and downs, life would start to feel flat and repetitive. If we never had to say goodbye, we'd never experience the joy of reuniting with loved ones. Without experiencing pain, joy wouldn't be as sweet because we'd have nothing to compare it to. The real beauty of life lies in its variety and its fleeting nature, making every moment precious.

Also, imagine being in a spiritual realm before our physical birth, fully aware of our connectedness and preparing to choose our lives on Earth. Would we opt for a safe and mundane existence, or crave something adventurous and unpredictable? Life on this planet allows us to experience both pain and pleasure, helping us find ourselves in the space between. We can feel the pain of separation from loved ones and then the joy of being reunited. Wouldn't we choose to explore every potentiality across time and space, versus staying in a heaven that never changes and is filled with unlived potential?

The story of my wife and me is filled with passion and challenges, crossing barriers of race, religion, upbringing, age, and tradition. We found each other when neither of us fully understood ourselves. Together, we faced many obstacles. There were times when it seemed too hard to go on, but our love and our beautiful daughter kept us going. We have a beautiful story because it wasn't easy. Our determination to hold on has been one of the most meaningful aspects of our relationship. If I could choose a perfect world where everything is unchanging, my first thought would be to always be with my daughter and my wife. But living in absolutes would have kept me from understanding the depth of our love.

It's separation that makes togetherness special. My wife and I love and adore our daughter to infinity and back. We've cherished every moment with her, from holding her as a baby to watching her grow. Even when she's at school, we miss her and dread the day she'll grow up and leave the house. But it's the fleeting nature of our time that makes our love so strong, turning each day into an honor and a blessing to be her parents. While we can't stop time or keep her young forever, we get to be part of the most beautiful journey we could ask for.

For many people, it's hard to understand why a perfect creator would design a world filled with conflict and tragedy. This question often arises when we face life's harsh realities—crime, wars, cruelty, sickness, and suffering. Yet, these challenging experiences enhance our capacity to seek justice, comfort, and kindness. This interplay of opposites isn't a sign of a flawed world, but a profound design where every eventuality can be lived and enjoyed.

In the grand design of existence, every experience enriches the whole of creation. By recognizing and embracing our dual nature as both distinct individuals and manifestations of the divine, we can truly grasp what it means to be human. This awareness helps us see that no bad moment exists without its good counterpart, allowing us to perceive life as a blessed experience.

Connecting Heaven and Earth

Just two weeks after I was born, my mother was diagnosed with terminal cancer at just thirty-three years old. Miraculously, she survived after enduring two grueling years of treatments, which were quite undeveloped in the 1980s. The aggressive chemotherapy and radiation, along with barbiturates prescribed afterward, altered her significantly. There was a lingering sadness and emotional distance, and as the years progressed, her mental state deteriorated. Though she was physically present, I felt her emotional and psychological absence. Family members often remarked that she was deprived of the joy of being a mother, especially during my early years, a time we never recovered.

During my early childhood, my aunt, after whom my daughter is now named, moved in with us to help raise me while my mother fought cancer. She stayed with me throughout my childhood and adolescence. Even though my mother and I shared a home, we were emotionally distant. I often wondered if she regretted not being able to mother me as she wished. There were many conversations we never had, and as time went on, the opportunities to connect slipped away as her mental state continued to decline.

Just before my mother's fifty-eighth birthday, the discovery of a benign brain tumor marked the start of another two-year battle. I was twenty-seven at the time. The first year involved several surgeries and numerous 911 calls, while the second year saw her mostly confined to the hospital. She suffered seizures, lost her hair, was unable to speak, and was fed through a tube. Watching her illness progress until she passed away was incredibly difficult.

Her passing after such a long fight left me with a deep sense of injustice. She had endured so much—fighting cancer twice, missing out on the full experience of motherhood, and passing away far too young. It was hard for me to reconcile the cruelty of the world with the idea of a benevolent God. During this period, I struggled to be present in work and relationships, felt detached from my body, and was tormented by my thoughts. From all angles, life itself seemed profoundly unfair.

For many years, I held onto inner resentment against God or the universe, feeling that life was rigged and filled with pointless suffering. It wasn't until my daughter came into my life that I could let go of the pain and resentment that once seemed never-ending. It's hard to put into words, but it feels like the same spirit that moved within my mother now moves through my daughter, playing out all the scenarios my mother and I longed to experience together. The roles are reversed—I am the parent, and she is the child—but the love we share does not feel new. In my relationship with my daughter, I find the love and connection I lacked with my mother.

Some would say that new life naturally heals past pain, but I believe it's more than that. My daughter's presence in this world doesn't just fill a void in my heart. It feels like we are the same spiritual entities, interacting in a world of symmetry, making up for the time I thought was lost. It's not just plugging any gap, but specifically the one between my mother and me. Many parents feel their children help heal their own childhood wounds, but for me, I sense that my daughter and I are continuing the same story, taking on different roles, like the same song played in alternate tuning.

This feeling of spiritual connectedness has brought healing to my heart and soul, teaching me that the lines between life and death are not as distinct as they seem. I believe in reincarnation, but I don't claim to understand how it works. Maybe my mother's soul lives in my daughter now, or perhaps just a part of it. It's not something to worry about. Life moves in cycles. We observe these cycles in the natural progression of the seasons, in how a seed sprouts into a tree, blooms, and eventually sheds seeds to create life again. We also see it in the orbits of planets and stars, and in our incarnations here. We can't always see the cycles for what they are, but we live within them.

The Cycles of Reincarnation

Matias de Stefano, an Argentinian spiritual teacher, claims to recall all his past lives and the intervals between them. His talks resonate with me deeply. He shares insights about the soul, the cosmos, and our interconnected existence. What's particularly interesting is how he provides specific information about ancient civilizations, shedding light on previously unknown aspects. For instance, Matias discusses how the ancient Egyptians viewed the Nile River as a representation of the human spine, with various temples along the Nile corresponding to different chakras or energy centers in the body. His detailed memories help bridge the gap between ancient wisdom and modern understanding, making complex metaphysical concepts more accessible and relatable.

Reincarnation isn't just a topic for mystics; it has also been studied scientifically. Dr. Ian Stevenson, a well-known researcher from the University of Virginia, focused on past life memories in children. Over his career, he investigated over 2,500 cases of children who claimed to remember past lives. He conducted in-depth interviews and carefully documented these children's stories.

Dr. Stevenson's research provided compelling empirical evidence supporting reincarnation and has brought significant attention to the topic in academic and scientific discussions. His work included detailed accounts of children who could recall verifiable facts from their alleged past lives, such as names, places, and events that they had no apparent way of knowing. One notable case involved a young boy who provided specific details about a previous life as a farmer in a nearby village. The boy accurately described the farmer's family, his house, and the way he died.

While the concept of past lives is fascinating, its significance diminishes in awareness, because past and future are only constructs of the mind. The universe is evolving, and our souls are participating in that journey, in varied forms, throughout time.

The Light and the Dark

As we've discussed, there are no absolutes except that which is absolute—the oneness underlying all things. All our experiences oscillate between endless dualities. We journey through light and dark, but it is the combination of both that makes up reality. Life has meaning because of death. Darkness allows us to understand the light. The light and dark can be seen as a metaphor for life, where light represents love, awareness, peace, and all that is good, while dark signifies the spirit of separation—of not knowing who we are, not recognizing our connection to something greater, and the presence of death.

We've talked about the importance of cultivating awareness to connect with something greater than ourselves, allowing us to live a more fulfilled and meaningful life. When we do this— often referred to as "raising your vibration"—we begin to see beyond the surface of our experiences and understand the deeper patterns at play. However, it's important to recognize that this process can sometimes bring challenges. As we raise our vibration, it can stir up unresolved issues and lower energies within us, bringing them to the surface for healing. This is why it's often said that it's darkest before the dawn. Just before a major breakthrough, we may experience some of our most difficult moments. But I want my daughter to know that these dark times are not a curse—they are the ladder she must climb toward the light. If she practices awareness, she'll see that the path toward the good things she desires often cuts through that darkness, and if she looks closely, she'll see opportunities hiding in plain sight. By holding onto this awareness and not giving in to despair, my dream is that she lives the best, most fulfilled version of her life she can. Darkness, then, no matter what shape it takes, is not a curse but a necessary step in our journey toward the light. I hope that is a comforting thought. Even death is not absolute, for in the end, everything returns to the one.

Since this book is inspired by my daughter, my last words in it are directly to her:

Dear Layla, my love for you goes beyond what words can express. In this world, we will not last forever. Death is an inevitable part of life. The thought of being apart from you seems too much to bear. But that's what makes our love so special. Awareness of our mortality allows us to see what holds the most meaning in our lives. Writing this book has been a part of embracing that truth. It is a profound honor to be your father in this lifetime. You and I will truly always be together.

Love,

Your Eccentric Father, Ali Kaden

www.ingramcontent.com/pod-product-compliance
Lightning Source LLC
Chambersburg PA
CBHW061328120726
48001CB00002B/742